About the Author

Daksha Patel is of Indian origin. She is a qualified Hindu. Born in October 1975, she has a BA Honours Degree in English with History. She also has a Post Graduate Certificate in Primary Education that includes Qualified teacher status.

Daksha is fluent in Gujarati and holds a purple belt in the martial art of karate.

Daksha Patel's motto in life is that if at first you don't succeed in your aims and objectives then you should try, try, and try again. Education is for character building and it enables us to shine like a star when we succeed at it.

The Modern Poetry of Daksha Patel

Daksha Patel

The Modern Poetry of Daksha Patel

Olympia Publishers
London

www.olympiapublishers.com
OLYMPIA PAPERBACK EDITION

A CIP catalogue record for this title is
available from the British Library.

ISBN: 978-1-78830-142-8

First Published in 2019

Olympia Publishers
60 Cannon Street
London
EC4N 6NP

Printed in Great Britain

Dedication

I dedicate this book to my family, my teachers and Swami Vivekananda, who is my role model. Also, a special thank you to my dear sister, Anita, whose funding has made this book possible.

Contents

Cobra

I have no arms,
I have no legs,
I smell with my tongue.
If someone harms me,
I hiss,
I raise my hood,
And inject,
My deadly venom.

By Ms Daksha Patel

Cobra Poem Comprehension

1. What is a cobra?

2. What is the onomatopoeic word in the poem?

3. What countries can you find cobra's in?

4. Is a cobra dangerous?

5. Are there different types of cobras?

6. Why does the cobra 'hiss' in the poem?

7. What happens when the cobra injects its venom?

8. Do people die from snake bites?

9. The cobra is a type of reptile. What does that mean?

10. How does the cobra smell things?

Cobras on a Rock

Notes on the Cobra Poem

The Falcon

The thunderous claws, keen to touch,
The ecstatic body of a moving machine,
Feathers of pride, puffed to heights,
Scanning like a radar.
The sudden wait…
Before a wondrous beauty takes flight,
A feast for elegant claws meets the sights,
While wings are pounding,
Beating the air,
A moving shadow casts,
Before a sunset,
He dominates earth and air.
The red sky sawn with a bullet.

By Ms Daksha Patel

The Falcon Poem Comprehension

1. What is a falcon a type of?

2. Can a falcon fly?

3. What feature does a falcon have?

4. How do a falcon's features help it to hunt?

5. Are there words in the poem that rhyme?

6. Which words in the poem rhyme?

7. Does the poem use metaphors in it?

8. Identify one metaphor in the poem?

9. Is the falcon's body compared to a machine?

10. What is meant by 'He dominates earth and air'?

A Flying Falcon

Notes on the Falcon Poem

An Alcoholic's Poem

Pouring the bottle,
How wonderful the colour of autumn,
Comes so peacefully,
Like a conker snug in its prickly shell,
Feeling comfortable,
Cradling my brandy glass,
Curved in its womanly shape,
My hands are warm,
Like the gulp I take,
As I drink like a baby to its bottled milk,
Feeling as calm as a sleeping child.

Soon I am numb,
Carried to meditation,
Till there's no pain,
No crying from inside,
No more fighting, to struggle, choking.
To an almost heavenly weakness,
I give in,
To that final shot.
So beautifully to finally lay down, to rest.

By Ms Daksha Patel

An Alcoholic's Poem Comprehension

1. What is an alcoholic?

2. Whose view point is this poem from?

3. What are the colours of 'autumn'?

4. Are there any similes in the poem?

5. Where are the similes?

6. Are there any metaphors in the poem?

7. Where are the metaphors in the poem?

8. Is there a comparison in the poem of drinking alcohol to drinking milk?

9. Have you ever drunk alcohol?

10. What does drinking alcohol mean to you?

Alcoholic Drinks

Notes on An Alcoholic's Poem

December Time

Winter is here,
Christmas is coming,
Snow is falling,
And children are singing.

The aromas of food and wine
Linger in Christian homes.
While trees are bare outside,
But inside there is mistletoe.

Winter is here,
Christmas is coming,
Snow is falling,
And children are singing.

The Christmas trees shine through people's windows,
As houses are covered with lights and tinsel.

Winter is here,
Christmas is coming,
Snow is falling,
And children are singing.

The snow is like a blanket on the ground,
With snowballs, the people are fighting.

Winter is here,
Christmas is coming,
Snow is falling,
And children are singing.

By Ms Daksha Patel

December Poem Comprehension

1. What is this poem about?

2. What season is this poem dealing with?

3. Is it a 'White Christmas' in the poem?

4. Why are children 'singing'?

5. What is 'Mistletoe' for?

6. What are people decorating their houses with?

7. When the poem says that 'people are fighting', is it a good thing or bad thing?

8. Have you ever played with 'snow'?

9. Which part of the poem do you like?

10. Does the poem remind you of your Christmases?

A White Christmas

Notes on the December Time Poem

Haiku:
Beehive

Sweet scent of honey
Roaming the fresh morning air.
The bees hard at work.

By Ms Daksha Patel

Haiku: Beehive
Poem Comprehension

1. What is a 'Haiku'?

2. What is a beehive?

3. Is the smell of honey 'sweet'?

4. Is honey sweet to taste?

5. Why are the bees 'hard at work'?

6. Who makes the honey in the beehive?

7. Are bees useful?

8. Where in the poem is alliteration used?

9. Can bees harm us?

10. Have you ever been stung by a bee?

A Bee on a Flower

Notes on Haiku: Beehive Poem

Under the Stars

Tender is the night,
When Milky Way dust falls,
On tormented bodies.
Glittering under white moonlight.
These two faint shadows move,
Whilst a hundred galaxies move over them.
The moon and stars illuminate their moist skins,
Like saffron on a hot summer's day,
Visible is their coil of perfection,
With these two bodies intertwined.
Cool and silent is the night.
The sky is filled.
Millions of tiny stars sparkle,
Like eyes on a happy child.
Black velvet is the blanket holding the stars,
And calm is the air.
Until a shooting star travels
The serene night sky,
Leaving a trail of hope, in a wish.
Wishful are the two bodies,
Embedded in each other's hold,
When they make love under a velvet blanket.
These two pull each other's heart strings,
Like playing instruments,
Until both hearts are filled to the core.
These two bodies, could they be the 'emblems of love'
When love fills their precious veins,
To the point of no return.

By Ms Daksha Patel

Under the Stars
Poem Comprehension

1. What type of poem is this?

2. What is this poem about?

3. Have you ever written a love poem?

4. Do you celebrate St. Valentine's Day?

5. What is 'saffron'?

6. What is the whole poem describing?

7. What is meant by the 'point of no return'?

8. Why are the two bodies 'wishful'?

9. How many metaphors can you find in the poem?

10. Is the poem positive about 'love' or negative?

A Heart Shaped Candle

Notes on the Under the Stars Poem

Morning

Blue is the sky.
White is the light.
The sun rays shine
Ever so bright.
From the roof tops of houses in Devon
There lies heaven.

By Ms Daksha Patel

Morning Poem Comprehension

1. What is this poem about?

2. What colour is the sky?

3. What rhymes in the poem?

4. What rhymes with 'Devon'?

5. What words make the poem descriptive?

6. What does 'heaven' mean to you?

7. Do you have a special place that you like?

8. Have you ever been on 'a roof top'?

9. What is the weather like in the poem?

10. Have you ever been to 'Devon'?

Devon

Notes on the Morning Poem

Blue

Blue is the colour of the sky.
Blue is the colour of your eyes.
Blue is the colour of my jeans.
Blue is the colour of your blueberry jelly beans.
Blue is the colour of my potion.
Blue is the colour of the ocean.
Blue is the colour of my sapphire ring.
Blue is the colour that I can sing.
Blue is the colour of my room.
Blue is the colour of my broom.
Blue is the colour of my music.
Blue is one of the colours of the chameleon.
Blue is the colour of this poem.

By Ms Daksha Patel

Blue Poem Comprehension

1. Why is this poem called 'Blue'?

2. Have you ever written a colour poem?

3. Is there some rhyming in the poem?

4. What effect does rhyming have in the poem?

5. What is a 'chameleon'?

6. Can a chameleon change into other colours than blue?

7. Do you like the colour blue?

8. Do you like another colour than blue?

9. What is a 'sapphire'?

10. Can music be blue?

A Blue Ring

Notes on the Blue Poem

Rainbow Poem

R is the Red hot lava from a volcano.
O is the Orange colour of a satsuma.
Y is the Yellow when the sun is seen at a distance.
G is the Green grass that grows beneath our feet.
B is the Blue sky without clouds.
I is the Indigo-coloured waters of the Caribbean.
V is the Violet flowers that grow on islands.

By Ms Daksha Patel

Rainbow Poem Comprehension

1. What is a 'rainbow'?

2. Have you ever seen a rainbow?

3. What conditions do you need to get a rainbow showing?

4. Can it rain and sunshine at the same time?

5. What are the rainbow colours?

6. Can you find the rainbow colours in the poem?

7. What is a 'volcano'?

8. What is a 'satsuma'?

9. What colour is 'indigo'?

10. What colour is 'violet'?

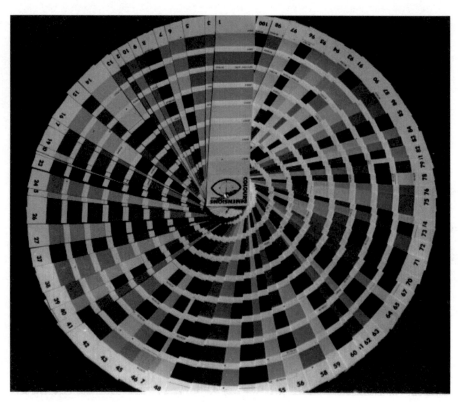

A Colour Chart

Notes on the Rainbow Poem

The Swan

With pure, pearly, white feathers,
The swan is a symbol of purity,
Of love and fidelity,
A mate for life.
This birdy can lay up to eight eggs.

With waterproof feathers,
And a streamline body,
This bird floats, dives, glides, and swims in water.
It looks like a white jet-ski on the water.

When searching for food,
Blessed is the swan with its
Webbed feet,
Long neck,
And strong beak,
For swans eat mostly vegetation.

Swans, they migrate to different places.
They have large powerful wings
To fly far.

On the regal and graceful white swan,
Sits Saraswati (the goddess of wisdom).
She rides the swan of royal and good qualities.
The swan's natural gift is:
To separate milk from water with its beak.
This appeals to the Hindu deity too,
For Saraswati tells us to discriminate between good and bad
And take only the good.

By Ms Daksha Patel

The Swan Poem Comprehension

1. What type of animal is a swan?

2. Where is there alliteration in the poem?

3. What is the swan compared to in water?

4. Why is the swan 'blessed'?

5. Who is 'Saraswati'?

6. What is the swan's 'natural gift'?

7. What does it mean to 'discriminate'?

8. What is a 'streamline body'?

9. Are all swans 'white'?

10. Why are swans a symbol of 'love'?

A Swan

Notes on the Swan Poem

Survival

'Africa!'
As the water falls from Victoria,
Comes the sound of the biggest cats in Africa.
The lions roar with the frightful sound of volcanoes,
While the Masai stand to protect their cattle,
But Masai shows courage and the lions respect,
So thundering on they go back to their pride.
The sound of a rhino in frustration is close.
The small cub of a lioness is lost.
And the laughter of hyenas never stops to rest.
In a land so full of mystery came
   The story of Anancy the Spider-man
     But all seems peaceful,
     Until the poachers come,
     They come to destroy harmony and peace.
     In search of ivory
     And furs.
     Blood covers Africa
     And from the
     Congo comes
     Fear for the
     Gorillas
     In the
     Mist!

By Ms Daksha Patel

Survival Poem Comprehension

1. What do you call this type of poem?

2. Do you know any other shape poems?

3. Is this a poem about the 'survival' of Africa's animals?

4. What is a 'poacher'?

5. Who are the 'Masai'?

6. Have you ever heard the 'laughter of hyenas'?

7. Who is 'Anancy'?

8. Is poaching moral?

9. What items come from poaching?

10. Where is the 'Congo'?

A Lioness

A Rhino

Notes on the Survival Poem

Me

In the morning, brushing my teeth white,
I clear the plaque.
I wash my face and body clean.
I dress the Hindu deity.
I ring a bell,
I light the diva and incense sticks.
I burn the camphor, and sprinkle water.
Then, I look in the mirror and see a reflection of me.
Me, me, not you.
In the afternoon, at school I read and write.
Scribbling on paper until it's right.
I do my sums and sit for exams and tests.
I study all I can for
Me, me, not you.
At lunchtime, I eat.
I chew, chew, chew the food in my mouth.
I eat for
Me, me, not you.
Then, in the evening,
I do my puja.
I light the lamp again,
It's a yellow flame.
I watch the television for
Me, me, not you.
At night, I sleep.
I dream of my day and me.
The bed sheets are as fluffy as snow and comfortable for
Me, me, not you.
There is nobody I would rather be than me!
This poem is about me and my day. It's about
Me, me, not you.

By Ms Daksha Patel

Me Poem Comprehension

1. Who is this poem about?

2. What is a 'Hindu deity'?

3. How is the day split up in the poem?

4. What effect does 'I chew, chew, chew' have in the poem?

5. What is 'puja'?

6. Do you have a daily routine like the one in the poem?

7. Who is important in the poem?

8. Is 'Me' a selfish poem?

9. What age do you think the author is in the poem?

10. Does the author like herself?

Daksha Patel

Notes on the Me Poem

Red

Red is the colour that angers and provokes the bull.
It is the colour of danger and warning.
Red tells us to stop!
It is the striking colour of style to dress in red
– To stand out!
Red is a lucky colour in Indian culture.
It is an auspicious colour for an Indian bride.
Red is the colour of fire, the sari of the goddess, Laxmi.
Red is the powder (called kumkum) used in marking the tilak on the foreheads of Hindus.
It is the colour of the great, red spot on Jupiter.
Red is the spot made from a laser pen to point out information.
It is the colour one sees when one is angry
– Red, red, red!

By Ms Daksha Patel

Red Poem Comprehension

1. What colour provokes a bull?

2. What is the main colour of danger and warning signs?

3. Do traffic lights turn red?

4. Does red stand out?

5. Is it good to write in red if you are Hindu?

6. What colour is the great, red spot on Jupiter?

7. What is 'kumkum?

8. Who is Laxmi?

9. What is an exclamation mark?

10. Where is there an exclamation mark in the poem 'Red'?

The Colour Red

Notes on the Red Poem

Hurricane Irma (2017)

Hurricane Irma was ever so firmer than Katrina ever was,
She smashed up houses and split up spouses,
Without a care in the world.

Irma created large floods,
Throwing debris including mud,
In the gusts,

She spilt some blood,
Regardless of age or creed.

Cuba, Antigua and Barbuda were some of those who faced Irma's wrath,
Regaining strength from the seas she was set to hit the Florida Keys.

Irma was the size of France,
The Americans evaluated this in advance,
Knowing her presence was near,
Most thought 'It's too dangerous to stay here.'

She flattened the Keys,
Leaving people crying on their knees,
But if they were in England,
Dot would be making them teas.

She left the people of Florida in tears,
Looking for their peers,
Exposed and bare,
With debris around everywhere.

Rebuilding will be hard,
But don't let down your guard,
Because hurricane Jose isn't afar.

By Ms Daksha Patel

Hurricane Irma (2017)
Poem Comprehension

1. What is this poem about?

2. What is a hurricane?

3. What countries did the hurricane Irma hit?

4. What happened to the people in the way of the hurricane?

5. What was Irma the size of?

6. Why would Dot be making tea?

7. What does Jose refer to?

8. How would you feel if you lost your property or even your loved ones in a hurricane?

9. What is the common poetic device used mostly throughout the poem?

10. Where would you go if you knew a category five hurricane was coming your way?

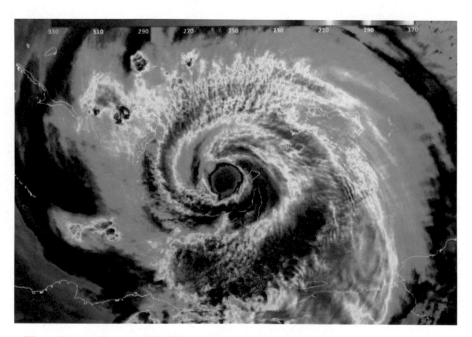

Hurricane Irma (2017)

Notes on the Hurricane Irma Poem

Mother Poem

Mother,
You gave me this body and mind.

Mother,
We share the same blood.

Mother,
You held me in your womb.

Mother,
For nine months I grew in you.

Mother,
You made me bloom.

Mother,
I love you dearly.

Mother,
I'll be old soon.

Mother,
In your footsteps I'll follow.

Mother,
I'll be as strong as you.

Mother,
I will always worship you as my Divine Mother.

Mother,
You are everywhere.

By Ms Daksha Patel

Mother Poem Comprehension

1) What is this poem about?

2) Whose mother is the poet talking about?

3) Do you celebrate Mother's Day?

4) What happens nine months in a mother's womb?

5) Do you love your mother?

6) What is meant in the poem when it says that 'I'll follow in your footsteps'?

7) Why is the mother 'strong'?

8) Does everyone have a mother?

9) Hindu's worship the mother. Why do you think that is?

10) Name one Hindu Goddess who is worshiped as mother?

A Hindu Goddess

Notes on the Mother Poem

Sweet Shop Poem

Humbugs are stripy like zebras.
Liquorice is black or red in long laces,
Cola bottles are like gummy bears and rings
– They are soft, clear and chewy.
Pick'n'Mix sweets come in all shapes, colours and sizes.

You suck the sweets down to zero.
Some are squishy and soft
While others are hard boiled and need some teeth.

Sweets defer in texture and taste.
Soft centred sweets ooze out with edible paste.
The juices race around your mouth when you eat sweets.
Especially, sweet and sour sweets.

There are no bitter sweets
But when you stand by the Pick'n'Mix there is a rainbow of colours
To entice children to buy those sweets.
Sometimes people even refer to me as 'sweet'.

By Ms Daksha Patel

Sweet Shop Poem Comprehension

1) Name some types of sweets from the poem?

2) What is Pick'n'Mix?

3) Do you like eating sweets?

4) Are sweets good for your teeth?

5) Why are sweets so colourful?

6) Name some of your favourite sweets?

7) What is the meaning of calling another person 'sweet'?

8) Name the shapes of some sweets you know?

9) Why do you have to suck some sweets?

10) Are sweets just for children?

A Selection of Sweets

Notes on the Sweet Shop Poem

Books Poem

Turning the pages and reading is like eating candy.
Each chapter becomes more tantilising and flavourful than the next.

The juicy words in the mouth roll around the tongue as I read the
autobiographies, adventure stories, poetry and science fiction.
Basically, I read whatever takes my fancy.

Each genre takes me on a journey to a new time and place.

While the encyclopaedias are a treat for finding delicious facts for my
projects,
Today, we have e-books as we move into the computer age where the
internet *rules*.

By Ms Daksha Patel

Books Poem Comprehension

1) Do you like reading?

2) What is your favourite poem?

3) What does the poet mean by saying 'reading is like eating candy'?

4) In the poem who is doing the reading?

5) What is your favourite genre?

6) Do you watch movies?

7) What is an e-book?

8) What is the difference between fiction and non-fiction?

9) Have you read a book that has been made into a film?

10) What can you learn from reading a book?

Books on a Shelf

Notes on the Book Poem

Haiku:
Apple Orchard

It is the ripe smell
Of apples that lingers in
The cold morning air.

By Ms Daksha Patel

Haiku: Apple Orchard
Poem Comprehension

1) What is an Orchard?

2) What is this poem about?

3) Identify a verb in the poem?

4) Identify an adjective that is used in the poem?

5) Identify one preposition word in the poem?

6) Do you eat apples?

7) Are all apples green?

8) Do all apples have seeds in them?

9) How do you know when an apple is rotten?

10) How many different ways is there to eat an apple?

Apples on a Tree

Notes on Haiku: Apple Orchard Poem

Sources/Bibliography

Books:
-The Children's Britannica.
-The Complete Encyclopaedia of Photography by Michael Langford.
-The Joy of Knowledge Encyclopaedia Books.
-First Poems by Robert Fisher.
-Poems for Thinking by Robert Fisher.
-In Search of God and Other Poems by Swami Vivekananda.

Internet:
-One Photograph is from www.shutterstock.com of Hurricane Irma.

Photographs:
-The Photographs are by Mr Dhanji Parbat Patel in this book.